PUBLIC SPEAKING:

The 30 Minute Quick Guide for Busy People

Learn How to Structure Your Presentation, Calm Your Nerves and Deliver an Amazing Presentation

ROMNEY NELSON

PUBLIC SPEAKING: THE 30 MINUTE QUICK GUIDE

© Copyright 2020 The Life Graduate Publishing Group
All rights reserved.

The content contained within this book may not be reproduced, duplicated or transmitted without direct written permission from the author or the publisher.

Under no circumstances will any blame or legal responsibility be held against the publisher, or author, for any damages, reparation, or monetary loss due to the information contained within this book. Either directly or indirectly.

Legal Notice:
This book is copyright protected. This book is only for personal use. You cannot amend, distribute, sell, use, quote or paraphrase any part, or the content within this book, without the consent of the author or publisher.

Disclaimer Notice:
Please note the information contained within this document is for educational and entertainment purposes only. All effort has been executed to present accurate, up to date, and reliable, complete information. No warranties of any kind are declared or implied. Readers acknowledge that the author is not engaging in the rendering of legal, financial, medical or professional advice. The content within this book has been derived from various sources. Please consult a licensed professional before attempting any techniques outlined in this book.

By reading this document, the reader agrees that under no circumstances is the author responsible for any losses, direct or indirect, which are incurred as a result of the use of the information contained within this document, including, but not limited to, — errors, omissions, or inaccuracies.

-Take Action Daily-
Life is too short to hesitate!

TABLE OF CONTENTS

INTRODUCTION	7
CHAPTER 1 – THE 7 MOST COMMON MISTAKES	12
CHAPTER 2 – EMBRACE AND ENJOY PUBLIC SPEAKING	24
CHAPTER 3 – THE A.V.A.T.A.R CHECKLIST	30
CHAPTER 4 – 5 EASY STEPS TO PRESENTING	35
CHAPTER 5 – THE HEART, HEAD, HAND, HEART TECHNIQUE	39
CHAPTER 6 – ENHANCE YOUR PRESENTATION WITH EFFECTIVE VISUAL AIDS	45
CHAPTER 7 – POSITIONING AND SEATING	51
CONCLUSION	

INTRODUCTION

I stood there looking out towards the 300 strong crowd. All eyes were fixed directly at me. There was a just light murmur as the audience felt my energy as I shuffled my handwritten notes at the lectern, ready to speak. I felt uncomfortable with the spotlight. I had nowhere to hide.

It was 1998, and I was conducting my first parent information night for the new cohort of students joining the school. I was the Year 7 Coordinator, and it was my responsibility to set the evening up for the school headmaster with an introduction to the year outlining what the students and families should expect for the next 12 months.

It was just my 2nd year of teaching, and my heart was in my mouth. Everything that could potentially go wrong had already played out in my mind 100's of times in the week leading up to the event. How this presentation would go would be anyone's guess!

I stumbled many times that evening with my words, my eye contact with the audience wasn't great, and the lack of preparation had become apparent. I realised if I were to become a strong future leader in the school and business, I needed to become a great public speaker. From that moment, I made it a goal to build my knowledge and, ultimately, my confidence in public speaking to take it to a new level. I needed to master the art of public speaking!

Hello, my name is Romney Nelson, and I am looking forward to providing you with an excellent resource that you can use from today forward. I'm uniquely positioned to write this book because my background is diverse and includes many years as a teacher, business leader, and workshop presenter.

I commenced my career as a teacher, and I taught for over eight years in leading Independent Schools across Australia and the

United Kingdom. I have held national executive roles of responsibility, and I have extensive experience as a presenter, coach, mentor, and facilitator across various educational and business forums.

I jump at the opportunity to present to large audiences, and it's because I've learned the essential skills and techniques to engage audiences. I intend to share these skills in a short 'power session' to accelerate your aptitude for public speaking and grow your confidence.

What Will We Cover?

There's no substitute for experience, especially when it comes to public speaking. What can significantly improve your capacity to become a great public speaker is by learning the structures and patterns that the best public speakers follow. I would describe it as a 'public speaking algorithm,' and once you learn the algorithm, you can continue to use that for any presentation you complete. The benefit of this book is that I'll break it down into simple steps and use language and patterns that can easily be memorized. Importantly, the way I teach public speaking involves simplicity and drawing on emotions. As American Poet and author Maya Angelou once said "I've learned that people will forget what you said, people will forget what you did, but people will never forget how you made them feel". Making your audience feel a particular way is like listening to a specific song that takes you back to your childhood or a special event. Even if you turned off the lyrics, the tune and rhythm of the song would make you feel a certain way. That could be happy, sad, angry, or relaxed. We want your presentation to make your audience feel a particular way and leave in a particular emotional state. What emotion you want to elicit to your audience is up to you, but emotions are the powerful tool we want to tap into when public speaking.

"I've learned that people will forget what you said, people will forget what you did, but people will never forget how you made them feel"

Maya Angelou, American Poet & Author

Chapter Breakdown

To help you on your journey, this book has been broken down into the following 7 areas.

Chapter 1
The 7 most common mistakes when presenting

Mistakes are a sign of progression, not a sign of regression. In this chapter, we identify the 7 most common mistakes that occur for public speakers, and we also discuss how to learn from those mistakes to become a better speaker.

Public Speaking might be regarded as the #1 fear for the majority of the population, but it doesn't need to be, and I'll show you why becoming a confident public speaker will allow you to earn more and elevate yourself to the top of your field.

Chapter 2
Embrace and Enjoy Public Speaking

As a starting point on your journey, it will be necessary to highlight why you should embrace public speaking and overcome any barriers you currently have.

Chapter 3
The AVATAR Checklist

This acronym is an exclusive method that only my students, both young and old, are taught and helps form your checklist for every presentation you ever do. If you can get a 'tick' beside the six elements of the AVATAR, you will deliver an excellent presentation.

Chapter 4
Five Easy Steps to Structure Your Presentation

In this chapter, I identify what steps you must master to allow your presentation to flow. I like to think of this as your public speaking foundation. Any robust structure requires a strong foundation that will remain stable and consistent to launch from. Building and tailoring a presentation specifically for your audience will deliver on the emotional element of public speaking. If you can build and then deliver on a well-researched, structured, and organized presentation, your audience will embrace it.

Chapter 5
The Heart, Head, Hand, Heart Technique

In this chapter, I introduce you to an excellent technique you can implement to easily remember the order in which you deliver your presentation, particularly if you have a 'call to action' for your audience.

Chapter 6
Enhance Your Presentation With Effective Visual Aids

For many of your presentations, a visual aid will play a pivotal role in amplifying and complimenting your message to your audience. Slides and other visual aids can also help with keeping to a particular topic, time format, and also help with creating a specific emotion through pictures, photos, videos, and music.

Chapter 7
Positioning and Seating

The seating configuration of your audience and the position of where you present can be critically important, but many underestimate how these two elements do impact the effectiveness of your presentation. In this chapter, we identify the different configurations according to the size of your audience, the type of presentation, the size of the room, and your intended interaction with the group.

To conclude, we look back over the main summary points for each of the chapters, and I provide a helpful checklist download that can be used to assist your presentations.

Learning the key points outlined in this book

will give you a huge competitive advantage across many different areas and can be one of the most powerful tools you can use to your benefit. Advantages of learning the art of public speaking include:

1. Greater productivity in meetings
2. Promotions for work and increase in pay
3. Better connection and rapport with your audience
4. Greater opportunity to deliver on areas you feel passionate about

Now we are ready to get started and accelerate your learning to deliver an amazing presentation!

Chapter 1

The 7 most common mistakes when presenting.

Most people look at mistakes and feel that it's a back-step in their progress; in fact, it's a sign of progression because we learn faster and grow stronger from our mistakes and failures than if things never went wrong. The same applies with public speaking and invariably, you will say things you shouldn't, miss the opportunity to say things that you should, speak too long or not long enough, have challenging audiences, have situations when the I.T stops working or your microphone goes silent right at a critical moment.

Yes, I've experienced all these things, but there are other mistakes that you can avoid if you prepare the right way. Below I have outlined the seven most common mistakes and how they can be avoided.

Mistake #1
Lack of Preparation

Even the most professional and experience of presenters rehearse and take the time to know their topic and have an understanding of their audience. You need to rehearse and say your speech out loud so you can get a feel for the tone of voice and know when to include pauses and suitably direct questions towards your audience. You also need to be prepared for potential questions from the audience.

Mistake #2
Arrive Late

You will be fighting to engage your audience immediately if you are late to commence. One key tip I provide during my lessons is to arrive early and welcome attendees as they enter the venue. Introduce yourself and make a connection before you even commence. Even better, try and remember 3 – 4 names and use these in the first 5 minutes. You will immediately commence your presentation with a huge amount of respect and provide an instant connection.

Mistake #3
Using Visual Aids Ineffectively

Visual aids are used primarily to support and enhance your presentation, but they can have the opposite effect if used ineffectively or incorrectly. Many people, even the experienced presenters, overuse their visual aids, and the message of the presenter can be lost. Many rely so heavily on their visual aids that when they strike a problem, they are unable to carry on as they have no back-up plan.

Mistake #4
Using Inappropriate Humor

You need to have a great understanding of your audience to be able to use many forms of humor. In a changing political and social world, many audiences have become sensitive to the use of humor in presentations. A joke may be interpreted the wrong way and could derail your presentation from the start or even sour the end of what may have been an excellent presentation.

Mistake #5
Not building a relationship with the audience

Connecting with your audience will enable your message to be delivered in a positive way. Without connection, your audience will simply disconnect, and nobody will listen. Worse still, ensure you don't simply recite or read word for word from your notes unless that is a requirement. If you do need to read directly from your notes, at a minimum, lift your head and make eye contact every few words. On this point, never announce that you are nervous or afraid. Some feel that this announcement will help them in the hope the audience will feel empathy for them. This is rarely the case, so commence without addressing your fear.

Mistake #6
Not using their voice correctly

A dull and boring voice will translate into a dull and boring presentation. You need to raise and lower your voice, pause, and create feeling in your words. It all relates back to how you make people feel, and the tone of your voice is an essential element. The 2nd element, is to ensure you use your voice appropriately when using a microphone or audio equipment. As there are different audio and microphone options available to speakers such as handheld, lapel, cordless, and attached, the speaker will need to be familiar with what is most appropriate for their presentation. You may also be limited by the options depending on the venue, it would be a mistake not to check well in advance of the presentation

The single biggest mistake of presenters is with handheld microphones. The most effective technique is to hold it at approx. 20cm or 8 inches from your mouth and lower the microphone, so the ball or top sits just under the chin level. This way, the audience can see your face, your voice tone is natural, and the microphone doesn't pick up any sounds from your clothing.

Mistake #7
Lack of Presentation Structure

A well-structured and organized presentation will flow and enable you to present with confidence and highlight the key points. Without structure, you may not deliver on your intended message and fail to create the emotional feeling that is important with any public speaking.

As noted earlier, it takes time, effort and clarity with your presentation structure to build your capacity to deliver on the public stage, but having a list of common mistakes, you can skip ahead of the pack and accelerate your public speaking expertise.

Chapter 2

Embrace and Enjoy Public Speaking.

Did you know that you are 15% more likely to be given promotions or management opportunities if you are confident with public speaking? Further to that, did you know that the same research suggests you can earn 10% more than those that fear public speaking! These are just two of the many reasons why developing confidence as a public speaker can provide you with greater opportunities that are far-reaching, not just for employment, but life in general.

Many will never get to the point of enjoying the center stage as a public speaker, but if I can move you closer to 'embracing' public speaking, then I feel that this is a huge step forward in your progression.

To help you to take that initial step if you do lack confidence or get nervous, let us look at ways that you can accommodate these emotions and take it all in your stride. It is also important to remember that being nervous is a natural feeling, regardless of experience, that we may all feel to varying degrees.

The 5 Keys to reducing anxiety, stress, and nervousness

Key 1. Prepare and Rehearse
Each time you have the opportunity to practice your presentation will significantly increase your confidence to deliver on the day. Never feel you can 'wing it,' regardless of your experience. If you don't rehearse, you are missing a huge opportunity to bring in the emotion and feeling of the message because you will be too focused on remembering what to say rather than how to say it.

Key 2. Breathing Exercises
When you get anxious, and your stress levels increase, you begin to restrict oxygen to the brain, and you don't think as clearly as you would if you were calm. To assist, begin by taking five deep and slow breaths by inhaling through your nose, so you really expand your chest and then exhaling out through your

mouth in a very controlled and rhythmic fashion. If it helps, bring your lips together like you were blowing out through a straw. Each breath should take you between 12 – 15 seconds to complete. You should start this breathing technique 15 minutes before your presentation and complete three cycles over a period of 5 minutes each.

Key 3. Visualization
Many people brush off the benefits of visualization, but I can tell you from over 25 years of experience that it is an untapped resource that I personally believe can increase the successful delivery of your presentation by more than 20%.
Visualization is a silent form of rehearsal and a great preparation tool. As an example, I complete 3 x 5-minute visualization exercises within 24 hours of any presentation or event. This involves sitting in a peaceful and quiet location, closing my eyes, controlling my breathing, and placing myself in front of the audience. I rehearse in my mind what I will

say in the first 2 minutes and imagine the warmth of the audience. By rehearsing in my mind the first 2 minutes, I feel greater confidence from the beginning, and this helps to get into the flow on the day right from the beginning.

Key 4. Move

There are two parts to this key tip.

Part 1 – Movement and activity before you present can reduce your stress and anxiety levels by increasing your blood and oxygen levels to your brain. If it is possible, complete a quick powerwalk 10 minutes before your presentation. If this is not possible, do 45 seconds of quick air punches. This will quickly increase your oxygen levels.

Part 2 – Some people find it more comfortable to hide behind a lectern when they present, but this can also have the opposite effect, especially for audience engagement. If the venue and your audio permit it, try taking a few steps from your central position or mingle with your audience.

Just ensure that your movement is natural and slow because too much movement can also distract your audience.

Key 5. Use Visual Aids

The use of visual aids is an excellent way to support your presentation, so the eyes of the audience are not squarely aimed at you 100% of the time. Visual aids will provide structure and prompt you to cover particular topics or key points that you can talk too, so you reduce the chances of forgetting important information. Remember that visual aids will 'support' your presentation, not 'be' your presentation.

Chapter 3

The AVATAR Checklist

There are certain techniques of learning that stick in your mind better than others. One of those techniques is by using a familiar word as an acronym where each letter will stand for a particular word or cue point.

I developed an acronym for my students that would be very easy to remember and memorable. The word was **AVATAR**. The word brings back memories of the highly successful James Cameron movie and is known across all age groups. This may be why this acronym for public speaking has been so well embraced.

Let's run through each of the letters and how they relate to delivering well on stage.

 = **Authentic**

Building trust with your audience can only be achieved if you are genuine and authentic. If no trust is established, your message will have lack credibility.

 = **Value**

Your presentation should never be all about YOU. The more you can involve your audience with questions and great eye contact, the better. You need your audience to feel they have gained value from your presentation, be that knowledge, skills, relaxation, excitement, humor, or entertainment.

 **= Audience**

Before presenting, know the kind of audience you are presenting to. Tailor your presentation or speech, specifically to that group. Try and obtain this information well in advance as each group will be different, and you need to adapt your delivery accordingly.

T = Time

Arrive early, keep to the allocated time of your presentation and respect the time of others. By respecting time, it will demonstrate your professionalism and add extra value to your presentation.

A = Audible

Words are powerful, and each word you speak will add value to your presentation. This highlights the importance of speaking clearly, projecting your voice, holding the microphone at the right distance from your mouth, avoiding monotone, pausing at the right moments, and ensuring that your audio has been checked before presenting.

R = Relevant

Have a clear understanding of your audience's 'needs' and 'wants.' Avoid straying too far from the topic or message and do your research to ensure you know the age, demographic, and requirements of the audience.

Chapter 4

5 Easy Steps to Structure Your Presentation

In this chapter, you will discover the 6 easy steps that you will use to build your presentation, so it provides the right flow from start to end. If you follow this structure, you will be using the exact method that many professional speakers use to build their own presentations.

Step 1. CAPTURE

By correctly capturing the audience's attention from the very beginning of your presentation, you immediately establish an expectation of what the audience will experience. This can be in the form of a story, a question, audience interaction, humor (if appropriate), a video clip, music, or an interesting fact. If you fail to capture the audience's attention in the first 30 seconds, you will be in an uphill battle unless you can elicit some form of emotional connection that can bring the focus back to your message.

Step 2. INTRODUCTION

Once you have captured the audience's attention, you need to outline the objective and how your information will benefit them. Similar to a book, if the author is unable to detail how the book will benefit you and outline what will be covered, you are unlikely to read any further.

Step 3. Body

The body of your presentation will contain all of the key information that you need to deliver. Each presentation will be different, but you may like to include the following elements:

- Facts and figures
- Statistics
- Expert testimonies
- Stories
- Historical background
- Case Studies and Real World Events

Step 4 – Call to Action

In this part of your presentation, highlight what the 'call to action' is. This will depend on your topic but could include the option to purchase a course, a resource, or an action that the audience are required to complete. This will not always be appropriate for all presentations but does play a key role, particularly in sales presentations.

Step 5 - Summary

In the final part of your presentation, you need to revisit the key parts of your presentation. You need to emphasize the 3 or 4 key points that are the most important. If appropriate, end with a story or information on how the audience can connect with you. Your summary will leave the audience with a very clear outcome and what value you have provided.

Chapter 5

The Heart, Head, Hand, Heart Technique

I want to introduce you to a fantastic technique that is not only easy to remember, but it is a brilliant technique that you can implement immediately. The technique uses body parts to structure your presentation to deliver on the most important element, EMOTION!

Let's now dissect each of the 4 elements and place them into a real-life example. We will use a presentation that a student that I coached used when he was preparing to present to the school leaders and peers at his school which ultimately resulted in him being elected as School Captain for the following year.

Heart

Your heart represents emotion. Start your presentation with a story or something that will generate emotion for your audience from the very beginning.

In the student's speech, he told his peers and staff of his memories of first starting at the school. He outlined how many amazing opportunities and memories the school had provided him over the past 6 years and the importance of giving back to the school to support future students. He also shared a story about how he had written on a piece of paper at the beginning of the year that his goal was to become a school captain and the significance for him.

Head

Your head represents the key information or the 'nuts & bolts' of your presentation. It could involve statistics, case studies, examples, etc.

For the student, he spoke about the times he had represented the school both in academic and sporting pursuits. He expanded on the importance of leadership in the school and what attributes a good leader should possess and why he would greatly appreciate leading the school and the students. He used this opportunity to demonstrate the qualities he had, and the students could then visualize him as their school captain.

Hand

The hand represents the call to action. It is at this time that you introduce an action that you would like the audience to complete.

The student outlined what his fellow peers needed to do in order for him to be voted as their next school captain. If they felt that he was a leader that would embody the values of the school and lead from the front, they needed to write down his name on voting day. He also subtly included his name at the end so the young students would remember who he was as there were another four students presenting after him.

Heart

The final step is to reintroduce emotion back into your presentation. You may recall at the beginning of this book that I said that people would not necessarily remember what you said, but how you made them feel.

The student spoke about the previous school captains and how they were amazing role models. He ended his presentation by thanking the students and teachers and showing his gratitude for the opportunity to be part of the school captain presentations. The audience could then feel how much he would embrace the opportunity and could feel his energy.

As this example demonstrates, the **Heart, Head, Hand**, and **Heart** technique brings together the key structural elements of a great presentation, and they are very easy to remember, regardless of experience. If you begin and end with emotion, your audience will be drawn to your presentation, and you will make a long-lasting impression.

Chapter 6

Enhance Your Presentation With Effective Visual Aids

Visual aids can significantly enhance your presentation, but only if used the correct way. Using them in the wrong way can be detrimental to the outcome and detract from your key message; therefore, I think it is imperative that I highlight 7 Tips to effectively use visual aids that will support your presentation.

Tip 1.
Minimalism

If using PowerPoint slides, the fewer words, the better. Avoid designing slides that are too busy and detract from what you have to say. Your slides should be 'cue points' that prompt you to introduce information, or alternatively, they should contain pictures or graphs, for example, that will best explain your message without the requirement for words.

Tip 2.
Color

The use of color can elicit different emotions. For example, green inspires interaction while red stimulates emotion. Colors can be lost, though, if you use the incorrect background color. For example, yellow on a white background can be hard to see from the back of a room but place yellow on a black background, and it is very easy to see. It is important, therefore, to choose colors that represent the information you would like to convey and the emotions you would like to evoke.

Tip 3.
Audience Size and Set-up

The choice of visual aids will depend on the size of your audience and the configuration of the space. Flip charts are more suitable for intimate or smaller groups under 50, while for groups larger than 50, consider PowerPoint or large projector screens that audience members at the back can clearly see.

The configuration of your room or the space of your presentation will also limit how you present your material. You may only have 30 people in the room, but if the space is long and narrow, then members of the audience at the back, they may not clearly see a flip chart. This highlights the importance of getting information on the venue or visiting prior so you can tailor your visual aids accordingly.

Tip 4.
I.T and Sound Checks

The compatibility of your computer file may not be suitable for the venue and the I.T equipment they have. I've been involved as an audience member on numerous occasions where the set-up will be configured for an Apple Mac, and the next speaker has their presentation on their own laptop. They spend 5 – 10 minutes trying to work out how to get the presentation onto the screen and precious time is wasted.

I would also highly recommend testing any audio prior to the presentation, especially for large venues. If you have a video or music to play, then test to ensure it works before and not when you are presenting. This can be of significant detriment to your presentation if the audio-visuals don't work as intended.

Tip 5.
Handouts

If you intend to provide handouts to the audience, I would suggest the following:

Groups under 30 – Appropriate to distribute at any time

Groups of 30 or greater – Distribute as attendees arrive, place on tables, on chairs, or request that attendees take one and pass on to other audience members no less than 5 -10 minutes before you present.

It is advisable that you don't initiate the distribution of handouts during a presentation to groups greater than 30, as this can disrupt the flow of your presentation.

Tip 6.
Whiteboards

If using whiteboards, ensure they are free from any previous information and clean. You will look underprepared and unprofessional if you start clearing previous notes in the middle of your presentation. Worse still, if you are unable to remove the previous information as they have used permanent marker pens!

When writing, use big and bold text and only use 3 to 4 different colors maximum.

Tip 7.
Back-up

Visual aids can have the uncanny ability to malfunction at the most inappropriate moments. Ensure you carry a back-up of your presentation on a spare USB and print off your slides before the presentation and keep to the side if you have specific information that you need to refer to.

Chapter 7

Positioning and Seating

There are generally 4 – 5 different configurations that you will need to familiarize yourself with depending on the presentation you will give.

These presentations could include:
- *A lecture or seminar*
- *A board meeting*
- *Workshop*

Keynote presentation

It will also depend on the size of the group, your relationship with the audience, your intended interaction, and the length of the presentation. Knowing these things will enable you to choose the most suitable layout if that is an option available to you.

The most common seating configurations are:

Theatre or Auditorium style:

Elevated and tiered seating. Great for noise projection but challenging for audience interaction if your intention is to move around the room.

Conference Style: This configuration is found generally in boardrooms and company meetings. The speaker usually positions themselves at the front of the room, and this configuration is more suitable to groups of 10 – 15.

U-Shaped: This configuration is great for workshops as the speaker can easily move around the room and encourages the speaker to interact with the group. This configuration is very good for audiences of 10 – 30.

Classroom Style: This configuration is one of the most familiar and encourages interactions with the audience. The disadvantage of this configuration is usually the lack of elevation for attendees at the back; therefore, it can be difficult for them to see any visual aids. If the speaker walks to the back of the room, they need to ensure they continue to project their voice at all times.

On Stage: This configuration usually has the presenter on an elevated stage so the audience can easily see them. Attendance numbers for this configuration can be in the low 20's to over 100,000. This configuration provides limited, if any, opportunity to interact with the audience depending on the size and access from the stage to the audience level.

With the variety of configurations available, you need to know what will work best for your audience and the information you need to deliver. In some situations, you will not be given a choice, and this highlights why knowing the venue before the day of presentation is really important so you can develop your presentation and visual aids appropriately for maximum impact and interaction.

Conclusion

The intention of this quick guide was to capture the key elements that will accelerate your success in delivering presentations in public speaking forums. Your capacity to deliver quality presentations will be a combination of test & trial, developing a robust structure that you are comfortable with, creating visual aids that compliment your presentation, and, most importantly, learning the skills to deliver the words that create the intended emotion.

To summarize what you have learned from this book, let's run through some of the key components across the seven chapters.

- Public Speaking is a brilliant skill to develop. It can be greatly beneficial for the workplace, for your personal brand but also to better communicate things that you feel strongly about.
- A great public speaker is able to weave both non-verbal and verbal

communication into their presentation. They capture the attention of the audience from the start and have the ability to create emotion with their words and visual aids. Use the Heart, Head, Hand, Heart technique when presenting.
- Prepare, Prepare, Prepare! Know your audience, rehearse your presentation, tailor your visual aids, and always have a back-up plan if things don't go to plan. Ensure you have structure and flow with your presentation.
- Obtain details of the venue. This will dictate if you will be able to include audience interaction based on the configuration, the visual aids to include, and what audio equipment you will have access too.
- Involve your audience by using appropriate eye contact and ask questions to generate strong engagement
- Know your audience – Who are you speaking too. By tailoring your presentation to the audience, you can

deliver the intended value.
- Take your time when speaking and keep the pace natural.
- Nerves are good, so learn to embrace them!

Thank you for reading the ***30 Minutes Quick Guide for Busy People***, and I hope this information will greatly assist as a reference point for your future as a public speaker.

My Free GIFT for You

To get you started, I have created a Public Speaking Guide booklet that you can print off and use containing many of the things we covered in this quick guide. To grab your free copy, please click on the link below.

Visit the following link to download it.

https://thelifegraduate8265.activehosted.com/f/17

The 30 Minute 'Quick Guide' Series

Available through all major online bookstores in eBook and paperback format.

PLEASE LEAVE A REVIEW

Thank you for reading the 30-minute guide. My aim is to provide great information that will help as many people as possible. The way you can help and to positively impact others is by leaving a review, thus, in turn, spreading the word so others can improve their lives. I read every review I get, and it helps me to make improvements and also know if you love my books.

About the Author

Romney is an Amazon Best Selling Author and the founder of The Life Graduate Publishing Group.

He represented Australia in the World Championships in 1988 in Dragon Boat Racing; he is a business coach, motivational speaker, qualified teacher, author and owner of two rapidly growing businesses in the educational space.

Romney has dedicated the past 20 years to helping others achieve success and fulfilment in their lives through his coaching, teaching, masterclasses, mentoring, resources and books. His clients speak of his passion and dedication for self-improvement and bringing that knowledge and experience to help others achieve what they want in their lives.

Romney is a sought-after speaker and is regarded as one of the leading experts in goal setting and daily habits with the development of the unique Dr ACTION™ and 'The Goal Loop' systems. He has a Bachelor of Education in Physical Education, is a qualified Personal Trainer and has previously held Head of Faculty positions in some of the most prestigious schools in Australia. He has also held senior executive positions in several Australian businesses.

Additional Books

www.ingramcontent.com/pod-product-compliance
Lightning Source LLC
LaVergne TN
LVHW041544060526
838200LV00037B/1128